QUEENHO

A Poem for the Queen's
Platinum Jubilee 2022

Simon Armitage

POET LAUREATE

faber

I

An old-fashioned word, coined in a bygone world.
It is a taking hold and a letting go,
girlhood left behind like a favourite toy,
irreversible step over invisible brink.
A new frock will be made, which is a country
hemmed with the white lace of its shores,
and here is a vast garden of weald and wold,
mountain and fell, lake, loch, cwm.
It is constancy and it is change:
the age of clockwork morphs into digital days,
but the song of the blackbird remains the same.

II

Queenhood: a long winding procession
from the abbey door to the abbey door.
Queenhood: vows taken among bibles and blades,
beneath braided banners and heralding horns;
the anointment of hand, breast, head, with oil
of cinnamon, orange, musk and rose; promises
sworn in secret under tented gold
so daylight won't frighten the magic away,
too sacred by far for the camera to see.
It is an undressing first then a dressing up,
a shedding of plain white cloth then the putting on
of a linen gown and the supertunica – dazzling gold foil
lined with crimson silk. Man will walk
on the moon, great elms will fail and fall.
But a knife's still a knife. A fork's still a fork.

III

So the emblems and signs of royalty are produced:
the gilded spurs; the blued steel sword – like a sliver
of deep space drawn from the scabbard of night –
to punish and protect; bracelets to each wrist,
sincerity and wisdom – both armour and bond.
Love is still love is still love, and war is war.

IV

And indestructible towers will atomise in a blink.
The God particle will be flushed from its hiding place.
The sound barrier will twang with passenger planes.
Civilisation will graft its collected thoughts
onto silicon wafers, laureates will trip through court . . .
But Taurus, the bull, on its heavenly tour,
will breach the same horizon at the given hour.

V

Queenhood: it is the skies, it is also the soil
of the land. It is life behind glass walls
and fortified stones. Robe and stole are lifted
onto your shoulders – both shield and yoke.
Motherhood and womanhood will be taken as read.
'Multitasking' will be canonised as a new word.

VI

It is an honouring, but also an honour.
In the flare and blur of an old film
ghostly knights and chess-piece bishops deliver
the unearthly orb, with its pearled equator
and polished realms, into your open palm;
and pass you the sceptre and rod of mercy
and justice, one bearing the cross, one plumed
with a white dove; and load your fourth finger
with a ring that makes you the nation's bride;
and offer the white kid glove with its scrollwork tattoo
of thistles and shamrocks, oak leaves and acorns;
then finally furnish your head with the crown –
jewelled with history, dense with glory –
both owned and loaned at the same time.

Do those burnished relics still hold
the fingerprints of a twenty-seven-year-old?

VII

A priceless freight for a young woman to bear,
but, draped and adorned, a monarch walks forward
into the sideways weather of oncoming years.
And the heavy cargoes of church and state
lighten with each step, syrupy old gold
transmuted to platinum, alchemy redefined.
Queenhood: it is law and lore, the dream life
and the documentary, a truthful fantasy.
For generations we will not know such majesty.

First published in 2022
as a signed limited edition
by Faber & Faber Ltd
Bloomsbury House
74–77 Great Russell Street
London WC1B 3DA

Typeset by Hamish Ironside
Printed and bound by TJ Books Limited, Padstow, Cornwall

A CIP record for this book is available from the British Library

ISBN 978–0–571–37960–6

FSC
www.fsc.org
MIX
Paper from
responsible sources
FSC® C013056